MOVING TO MC

Creating a successful remote
work environment

MOVING TO MOBILITY

Creating a successful remote work environment

Catherine Roseberry

Business Information

First published in the UK in 2008

by
BSI
389 Chiswick High Road
London W4 4AL

© British Standards Institution 2008

All rights reserved. Except as permitted under the *Copyright, Designs and Patents Act 1988*, no part of this publication may be reproduced, stored in a retrieval system or transmitted in any form or by any means – electronic, photocopying, recording or otherwise – without prior permission in writing from the publisher.

Whilst every care has been taken in developing and compiling this publication, BSI accepts no liability for any loss or damage caused, arising directly or indirectly in connection with reliance on its contents except to the extent that such liability may not be excluded in law.

The right of Catherine Roseberry to be identified as the author of this Work has been asserted by her in accordance with sections 77 and 78 of the *Copyright, Designs and Patents Act 1988*.

British Library Cataloguing in Publication Data

A catalogue record for this book is available from the British Library

ISBN 978-0-580-50727-4

Typeset in Akzidenz Grotesk and Minion by Helius, Brighton and Rochester
Printed in Great Britain by MPG Books Ltd, Bodmin, Cornwall

Contents

Introduction vii

1 Management overview 1

2 Remote offices 13

3 Working comfortably – ergonomics, background noise
   and other considerations 27

4 Communication 33

5 Using the Internet 41

6 Making connections 49

7 Security 59

8 All the right gear 75

9 Software 99

10 Successful remote working – a conclusion 113

Introduction

Remote workers are not a new phenomenon that occurred because of the increased and inexpensive availability of the Internet. Remote workers have been around for hundreds of years – tinkers, gypsies and the infamous 'travelling salesmen'. They and all other professionals who travel as part of their work are remote workers.

While the advances and improvements in mobile equipment have made life easier for remote workers, they have also created new challenges that did not previously exist. In years past, it was enough to have a pocketful of coins for telephone calls and a sturdy case full of documents while on the road.

Advancements in technology now enable remote workers to work from practically anywhere in the world. Learning how to work properly with these technologies can give remote workers advantages over those working on site but it is important for remote workers to properly manage and use these technologies. Managers also play an important role in the success of any remote work programme, as they must establish the ground rules for remote workers and create guidelines to enable the success of a remote work environment.

This book will provide remote workers with information, and enable remote work managers to help remote workers, to make informed choices about the way they work, where they work and what equipment is best suited to fulfil their job functions. This information will help them maintain and in some cases improve productivity while working remotely.

Many books and other resources on remote work have been prepared from an academic perspective, and very few cover topics specific to what mobile equipment is required, how to use technology for remote workers and the role that management can play in successfully overseeing remote workers and the technology they require. Issues such as communication methods or security issues are often covered briefly or covered either in a highly technical perspective or for a non-professional home user.

This book approaches subjects in ordinary language and explains the technical terms in plain English, so that a manager or remote worker at any level can understand and put this information immediately to use.

Remote workers and companies who wish to take advantage of the technology available and how best to make it work for them will find this book beneficial. This book can be used as a training resource for new remote workers to guide them to successfully work in a remote work environment and for companies to improve the performance of existing and new remote workers.

Management overview 1

Managing remote workers involves a different mind-set from working with employees on site. It is important to understand what is required to successfully manage remote workers and how to create successful policies and agreements.

The right mind-set

Whether you already have a remote work programme in place or you are contemplating beginning a remote work programme, you must first understand what you hope to accomplish and what your objectives are for allowing your staff to work remotely. Remote work has a variety of benefits, of which just a few can include improved customer service, improved employee morale and potential savings related to office space and resources. Considerations for remote work can also include government legislation aimed at improving or providing better work/life balance, for example the Work and Families Act 2006 in the UK, which provides for greater flexible working, and the Federal Employees Flexible & Compressed Work Schedule Act (FEFCWA) in the US, which enables federal workers to have a wider choice in the way in which and the location from which they work. Other European countries such as Sweden, Czech Republic and Germany are known to have successful remote programmes in place.

Managing remote workers requires a different way of thinking and looking at work. You cannot check an employee's desk to see how many files are completed or to see that they really are working. Remote work involves investing trust in the people you have selected to know that they are working and to the best of their ability with the tools provided.

It is important that remote work is not used as a method of unfairly distributing work, or as a means to pay workers less simply because they are not on site.

Remote work managers should also be capable of thinking creatively and know how to evaluate a worker (especially true in the case of a remote worker) based on the quality of work and the positive feedback received from customers and co-workers. There may be work completed that can be measured and quantified, though this may not always be the case.

Managers and remote workers must all be aware that remote work policies and agreements are legal documents and are to be adhered to. Consequences of violating terms of the policy and/or agreement should be made available to all concerned.

Selecting remote workers

In selecting remote workers, managers should not rely on personal likes or dislikes. This will result in the selection of personnel who are likely to

1. MANAGEMENT OVERVIEW

be unsuitable for remote work but are instead rewarded for being friends with or close to management. When determining the suitability of an individual for remote work, the criteria should be evaluated with an unbiased perspective. Evaluation by committee, based on a predetermined list of criteria, is the most logical and fairest method to select remote workers.

Two methods can be used for selection:

1. Selection is decided entirely by management, and the potential remote worker is then approached.
2. A system can be set up to allow employees to apply for remote work consideration. If the application method is used, all employees within positions that are suited to remote work are informed of the selection process. In addition to completing an application for consideration, there should also be a set time for determining eligibility and when management will provide a response.

It is worthwhile to keep reminding yourself that not all employees are suitable for remote work and, while many may desire to work in a remote work environment, the reality is that it takes a skill set that not all possess and some cannot learn.

Selecting the potential remote workers who can be successful should be based upon evaluating characteristics that reflect on work and overall personality traits and behaviours.

Ideal remote work characteristics

The ideal candidate:

- is self-motivated;
- is results-oriented;
- is able to set and meet deadlines;
- is reliable and responsibly completes work duties;
- not only understands their position fully but the part their position plays in the company;
- is comfortable working independently with minimal or no supervision;
- is an effective communicator;
- adapts well to changes in job functions, routines and environments;
- has spent enough time in their respective position and is deemed fully trained;
- is highly motivated to do their best for the company;
- is trusted by supervisors and management;
- demonstrates strong skills in prioritizing their duties and managing their time;
- has received positive performance appraisals, which show high proficiency in their position.

Remote work policies

Remote work policies are a general overview of the programme and set out what a company expects from their remote workers. More detailed clauses and specific situations are included in a remote work agreement. A company's remote work policy will be specific to their own situation and many templates are available on the Internet that can easily be adapted.

Beginning a remote work programme without a policy in place first can be very risky. Determining responsibility or specific job functions can be difficult after a remote work programme has begun. Job functions and responsibilities should be clearly defined for both the remote worker and their supervisors, before any remote work programme is initiated. Creating the initial remote work policy should be a joint effort between management and potential remote workers. Working together as a team to create this document will help ensure that important details are not forgotten and may bring up other issues that should be included. As a side note, if there is a trade union involved with the workplace, then a union representative should definitely be present, as in most cases the union will have concerns that will need to be addressed in a remote work policy. These may run the gamut from salary considerations and mandatory remote work requirements to working hours and availability.

If you do not have a remote work policy in place, it isn't too late to create one and put it into force. This is for both management's benefit and that of the remote worker.

Why is it important to have a remote work policy?

The policy sets out rules that apply to all remote workers and management. It enables both sides to know and be aware of their responsibilities for the success of a remote work programme. A remote work policy should cover potential situations that may arise with remote workers and their managers before they happen and detail how they should be handled.

Managers should stay on top of their remote worker's performance and be ready to take action should the performance drop below a predetermined standard. A remote work manager should also maintain proper communications so that they are aware if there are issues that are affecting the performance of a remote worker. Managers must be able to quickly respond and handle issues that arise without creating more problems.

The biggest roadblock for most who manage remote workers is accepting that, in many cases, workers are more productive when working remotely.

What should a good remote policy contain?

- A remote work policy should begin with an explanation of the criteria for remote work opportunities. For example, that employees must have held their position for a specific period of time or completed specific training courses, etc. Not all jobs can be fulfilled in a remote work environment and spelling out which jobs will meet this criteria will prevent problems from occurring later.
- The policy should also include what locations are covered – home offices, satellite offices, on the road, etc. Some remote workers may work from a combination of these locations.

1. MANAGEMENT OVERVIEW

- The policy should contain wording that specifies what type of contact and reporting methods will be in place.
- It should detail what expenses (if any) an employer will be responsible for and those for which remote workers have responsibility. This could include a one-off reimbursement for home office furnishings or equipment for a vehicle office. An amount should be specified for each situation.
- The policy should also contain a clause that covers confidentiality of work and what steps remote workers must take to protect their work. This can include physical and software security requirements for documents and equipment.
- The policy should also contain a general clause describing what equipment and other tools will be provided by the employer. This may be in addition to a detailed clause included in the remote work agreement.
- It should also detail acceptable and proper use of company resources including the Internet and mobile equipment.
- There should be an ownership clause spelling out what equipment and tools remain the property of the company.
- There should also be a clause detailing how a remote worker will be evaluated and when evaluations will occur.
- The policy should clarify the use of personal equipment in lieu of company-owned equipment. Security concerns may dictate that personally owned equipment is not to be used.
- The policy should also detail the level and availability of technical support available to remote workers (though it is advisable that

remote workers should be capable of basic to intermediate troubleshooting on their own, with training provided by the organization as appropriate).
- The policy should detail when mobile equipment should be brought in for updates and routine maintenance.
- There should be an explanation of office/equipment sharing arrangements when remote workers must work on site.
- The policy should detail responsibilities of remote work managers – this will include how they maintain contact with remote workers, report keeping, ensuring that proper support is in place for remote workers, etc.
- There should be a process for conflict resolution.
- There should be a clearly defined process by which both the remote workers and their managers can raise suggestions/concerns regarding the remote work programme. This open dialogue will allow everyone to feel comfortable to make improvements or change things that are not working.

Remote work agreements

A remote work agreement will be tailored to specific positions or personnel. It includes clauses that contain exact specifications for completing work and details the methods to be used.

A good remote work agreement contains the following.

1. MANAGEMENT OVERVIEW

- An agreement that identifies the remote worker and their position.
- Details of when the remote work arrangement begins, when it ends (if applicable) and how this arrangement can be terminated.
- A more detailed listing of mobile equipment and tools that are provided to a remote worker.
- Any pertinent legislation or union rules that apply to remote work arrangements.
- The work schedule and hours that the remote worker will be working and available to management.
- Specific methods of staying in touch with co-workers and management. These can vary depending on where a remote worker may be working.
- A description of specific home or vehicle office requirements.
- A home office inspection report – to verify safety and security precautions are in place.
- Details of a process for reporting any injuries or accidents that occur while in company time or in a company vehicle.
- Insurance requirements – the remote worker is responsible for insurance for personally owned property, home office furnishings and a personally owned vehicle. The company is responsible for any company purchased or owned items.
- Reimbursement details specific to a position. Not all jobs require the same expenses. This is a more detailed listing than the one included in the remote work policy.
- Contact information for the remote worker – main and alternative telephone numbers and email addresses.

- Details of specific equipment that a remote worker may be using outside of what has been provided by the company.
- Description of responsibilities if a vehicle will be used – including those for insurance, maintenance and fuel.

Guidelines for casual remote workers

Companies should have in place general guidelines for all employees who may on occasion work in a remote work capacity. Those who work one or two days per week from a home office are casual remote workers. They may be working from their home office due to inclement weather or because they are too ill to go into the office but not too ill to work. In these cases, the employee should notify their immediate supervisor to advise them of their situation. If they don't already have access to the company network for email or access to documentation, the supervisor can arrange for the employee to get that access. Most companies already allow employees to check email from locations outside the office so this should not pose any problems.

Any employee who has a position that can be fulfilled from a remote location (even if they don't work full-time in a remote capacity) should have guidelines that outline their responsibility for protecting company data, basic home office set-up requirements and procedures for reporting in while working from their home office.

1. MANAGEMENT OVERVIEW

Standard remote work agreements in place can be used with the pertinent clauses highlighted and those that do not apply can be removed.

Remote offices 2

What are remote offices?

A remote office may be a worker's home office, their vehicle or a satellite office. For any remote office set-up, it is important that companies set standards for what equipment will be required for these offices, who will provide the equipment and whether inspections will be required of these locations.

An important consideration for anyone using his or her own home office or a vehicle as office space will be to ensure that there is proper insurance coverage in place to protect against theft or damage. To ensure that the correct coverage is in place for a home office both the company and the individual should speak with an insurance specialist to make sure that privately owned equipment and company-owned equipment are each covered.

Home offices

How a home office is set up will be determined by the amount of time spent using it and the type of work done. Most remote workers using a home office will require the same computer equipment that they would have had access to in the corporate office setting. A properly furnished home office also ensures that a remote worker will be able to work comfortably and safely.

The bare minimum requirements are a desk, proper chair and secure storage such as a locking filing cabinet or safe. For any individual spending the majority of their time in their home office and minimal time on site, a desktop computer is often the best choice.

Tips for planning and setting up a home office

- It is preferable that the home office be located in a dedicated space – not a shared use space. If a shared space must be used, provide a means of privacy such as a screen or shelving unit as a divider.
- If your home office does not have a door that locks (most preferred option), a locking file cabinet or safe should be available to store storage media, program disks and confidential data.
- Lighting and ventilation are often overlooked when selecting a space for a home office. A window, which provides natural light and can be opened in agreeable weather, can make working conditions much more comfortable.
- Make sure there will be enough room not only for computer equipment but also for laying out work.
- Check that the electrical facilities will be able to handle the equipment. Upgrade if necessary.
- Count the number of plug and phone sockets that are available. It is much easier to add more of either before setting up the office furnishings.
- Draw up a layout to see that sockets will be used properly and the use of extension cords minimized.

- Plan home office space so that there is adequate room for storage of supplies and resource materials.
- A proper office chair is necessary for anyone with a home office. It is far better to get a good quality, ergonomic chair that will last and make you comfortable.
- Ensure that the desk or workstation has a work surface that is the correct height and provides adequate space.
- Measure furniture before trying to fit it into the space. New furniture or alternative ideas may have to be considered.
- Before committing to a particular arrangement of furnishings and equipment, take the time to try different layouts.
- As the office is arranged, keep lists of what equipment and furnishings were purchased privately and which are company owned.
- When setting up a computer monitor or positioning a laptop, keep in mind that there will be glare from windows or light fixtures. Arrange the display(s) so that glare from light sources will be minimized.

Vehicle offices

Prior to any company allowing their remote employees to use their vehicles as remote offices there should be clear rules regarding proper and safe use of mobile equipment while driving.

Vehicle office policies should be used for all remote workers who will be using a vehicle as an office. These will clearly define what is expected of remote workers while operating privately owned, rented or company-owned vehicles. It is the responsibility of all remote employees to know the laws regarding mobile phone use and whether it is unlawful to use a mobile phone while driving or if using hands-free kits are acceptable. Legislation regarding mobile phone use is changing frequently – employees should keep themselves up to date with any changes, as any fines or fees imposed will not be an allowable expense.

A company must also set in advance what expenses they are willing to reimburse for the set-up and use of vehicle offices. A company may provide a set allowance for initial set-up to cover purchase of storage and organizational containers. All remote workers should be made aware of what expenses they will be reimbursed for and which will be out of their own pocket.

Any remote workers who will be using their own vehicle should also check to see what type of insurance coverage they have for business use of their vehicle and what type of content coverage is in place. Special clauses or endorsements may be required to cover mobile equipment and material that is kept in the vehicle. These points also apply to company-owned or rental vehicles. Using the vehicle as a remote office does change the use of a vehicle and failing to have proper insurance coverage in place could be very costly.

Vehicles can be modified and set up to be used as effective remote offices without having to make major changes to them. The quickest method to provide easy storage for files and equipment is to use plastic totes, which can be fitted with file organizers, and smaller storage bins within a larger one. There are mobile work surfaces available, which can be installed to support a laptop computer and provide storage for files.

There is no ideal vehicle for a remote office – storage containers can be placed in trucks or secured in the back seat of most vehicles. What is important is that, whenever possible, remote workers should install their storage containers in the most secure manner possible. Bolts can be added to the bottom of storage bins to secure them to the floor of a boot or hatch space. Safety straps can also be used to hold storage containers in place.

All remote workers should be strongly advised to adhere to security precautions when using a vehicle office. Keep all documents filed and out of sight when not in use, the same goes for all mobile equipment that is in the vehicle. Doors and the boot should always be locked when away from the vehicle.

Satellite offices/shared offices

Satellite offices can be a branch office of a company or a business centre that provides computer and other office equipment for remote workers to use when they are too far from their corporate office or their home office. Some of the business services that may be provided at these locations include:

- faxing;
- photocopying;
- high speed Internet access;
- conference call facilities and services;
- private work areas;
- access to resource materials.

Shared offices are set aside within the corporate office as work areas for the shared use of the remote workforce, providing all the resources and equipment that on-site workers have available.

For both satellite and shared offices, remote workers may have to schedule or book time to have use of those facilities. There should be space provided for remote workers to secure their work, which they may need to store while away from the office.

Internet cafes/hot spots

Internet cafes and hot spots provide another option for remote workers to work while away from the office. It is important to note that these are not secure environments to work in and due care should be taken to ensure that no information or files can be taken and that workers do not leave their mobile equipment unattended.

These locations should be used as choices of last resort and only when there is no other option for Internet access.

Checklists for home office equipment and supplies

Furnishings

ITEM	QUANTITY	PERSONALLY OWNED	COMPANY OWNED
Desk/workstation(s)			
Chair(s)			
Filing cabinet(s)			
Bookcase(s)			
Table(s)			

Company-owned equipment

MODEL NO.	DESCRIPTION	SERIAL NO.	DATE RECEIVED	DATE RETURNED

Privately owned equipment

MODEL NO.	DESCRIPTION	SERIAL NO.	DATE PURCHASED & PURCHASE PRICE	WARRANTY DETAILS

Office layouts

The following diagrams offer some examples of good office layouts.

2. REMOTE OFFICES

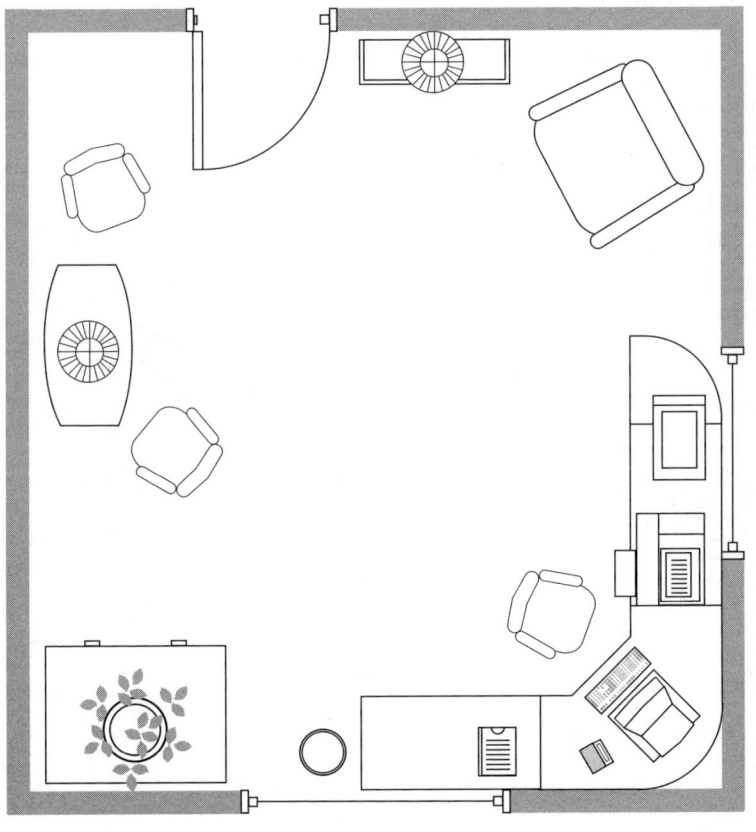

MOVING TO MOBILITY

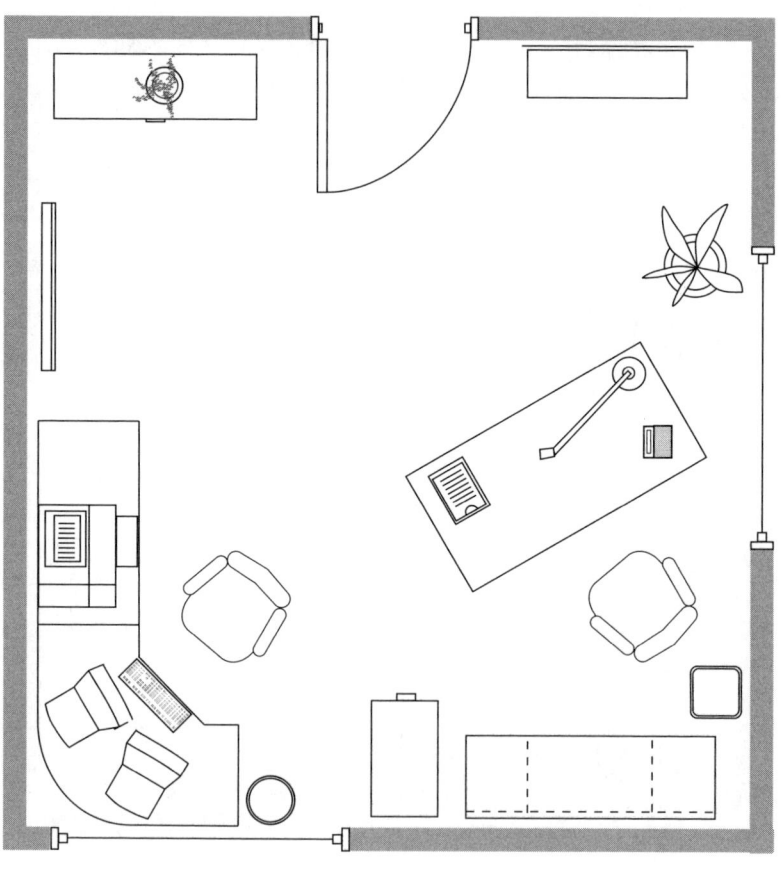

2. REMOTE OFFICES

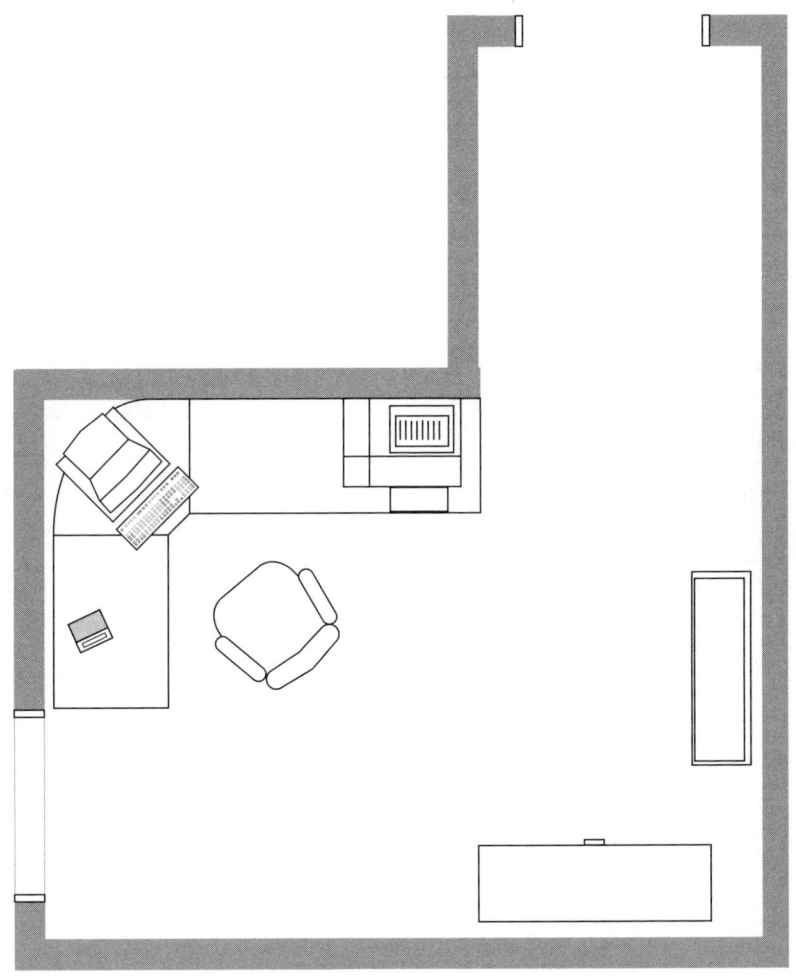

MOVING TO MOBILITY

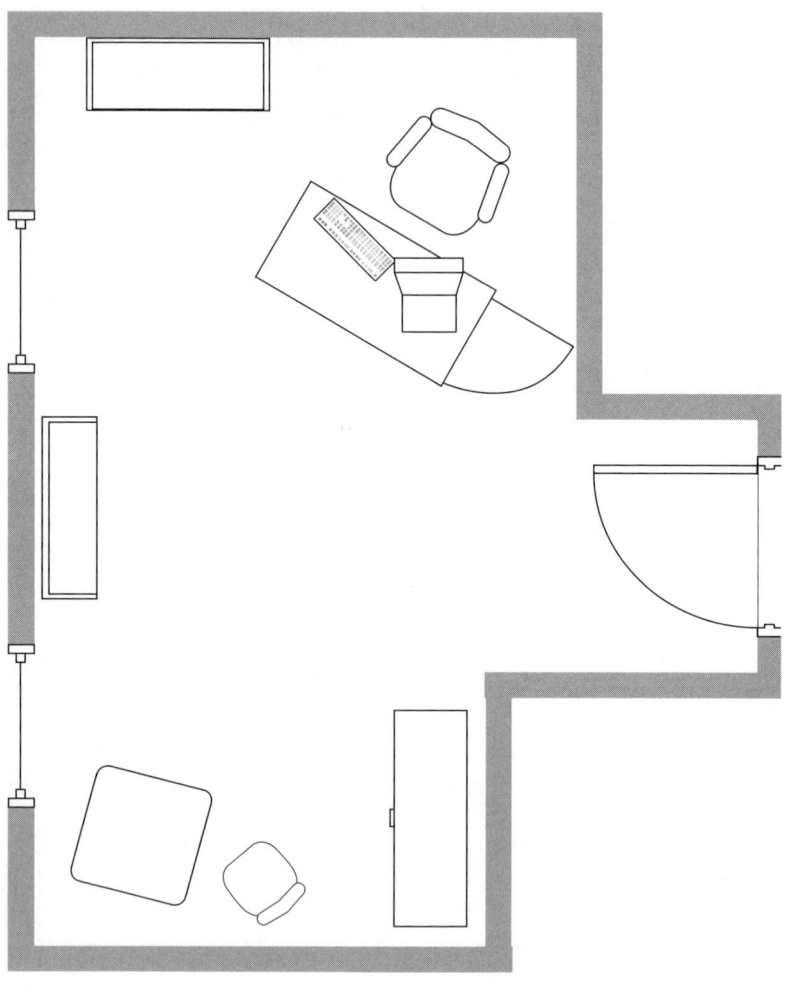

2. REMOTE OFFICES

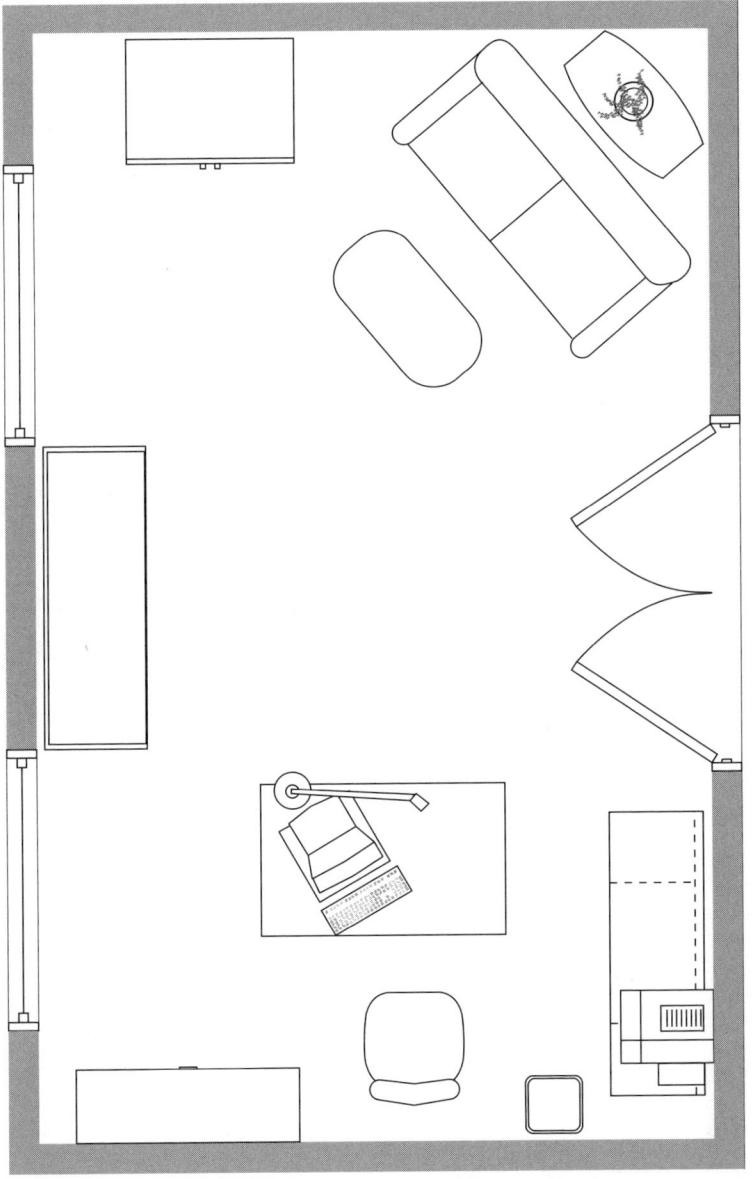

3 Working comfortably – ergonomics, background noise and other considerations

Background noise

It will not always be possible to control background noises while working remotely but it is possible to minimize the effect it can have while you are participating in a phone or video conference, during phone calls and while viewing presentations.

The first and easiest method to deal with background noise it to schedule your work to times of day when background noises are less likely to disturb you.

If you are working from a home office and there are other people home at the same time as your important phone call, explain to them why you need a quiet environment where you will not be disturbed and make sure that any televisions, radios and other noise-making devices are turned off if you can hear them from your office. This is why having a dedicated room for your office is such a great idea. You can close the door to cut down on noise interference.

If you need to make a phone call while on the road, be sure to first pull over and try to find a location that is away from the roar of traffic so that you can be heard and hear clearly.

In more public locations it can be trickier to prevent background noises so always try to find a spot that is well away from roadways, doors and places where music is played in the background.

Ergonomics – the art of working safely and comfortably

Ergonomics is something that remote workers may not consider or feel is very important but it can affect how well you work and how you feel while working.

Acquiring and using proper ergonomic equipment will help to ensure that you work in a safer and healthier environment. No matter where you happen to be working, you should always try to make sure that you are working as ergonomically as possible.

Home office

When setting up your home office, it can be tempting to use existing furniture such as dining room chairs and tables or other, improvised furnishings.

3. WORKING COMFORTABLY

While it may be more economical initially, in the long run your body and your productivity will be affected and you will find it harder to get quality work done unless you invest in proper office equipment that is designed for the purpose.

Your work surface should be at a comfortable height that allows you to view your monitor at eye level. You should not have to strain to view your monitor – even for laptops. A wide variety of adjustable monitor risers are available that allow you to find the best height for your monitor.

If you regularly use a laptop rather than a desktop computer, invest in a laptop stand (or laptop riser as they are also known). This little gadget will not break the bank but will prove invaluable to your health and comfort. Look for a laptop stand that can be used on a desktop surface, on your lap and above all provides excellent ventilation so that heat is dissipated from your laptop.

Once you have a work surface that is the correct height for you, your office chair is the next most important piece of furnishing. Go to a store and try out different chairs whenever possible. Research the different styles of chairs available to see which will suit your needs best. Leather chairs sound great in theory but can become very hot and uncomfortable to sit in for long periods of time.

The layout of your accessories such as printers and scanners should also be planned. You want to be able to easily reach these items and not overextend or contort yourself just to reach the printer or scanner.

As someone who worked at a makeshift desk and used a regular dining room chair, I know that my back, neck and shoulders all appreciated the switch to an ergonomically designed desk and proper office chair.

Vehicle offices

Just because your office is on four wheels does not mean that ergonomics are not an important factor. We all know that it is not a good idea to do any work while driving but it is possible to set up a stable work surface for when the vehicle is not in motion or you are a passenger.

There are laptop work surfaces that can hold files, a printer and supplies that sit on the passenger seat or in the space between the driver's seat and the passenger seat. There are also floor-mounted laptop stands, which provide a stable and secure surface for your laptop.

Satellite office/hotel rooms

In this scenario, you may not have a great deal of choice as to the work surface or chair provided. Do try to pick the work area that provides the best ergonomic set-up and which can be adjusted to suit your personal needs.

Many hotels are now spending more time and money to provide ergonomically designed work areas in hotel rooms. They realize that this can be an important factor for remote workers to consider when selecting a hotel.

Making the right choices regarding ergonomics from the start of your remote work journey will pay off in the long run as you will have fewer aches and pains, better productivity and a better work flow.

Other health considerations

While it can be tempting to work long hours and get the most work done at one time, it is important that remote workers remember to take regular breaks to stretch and loosen up muscles in order to prevent repetitive strain injuries, eye strain and other health problems.

When working on site, breaks are a normal part of the workday and even unscheduled breaks such as chat time with co-workers around the copier or water cooler is expected; it can be hard to remember to take the same number of breaks when you are working remotely.

If you have a hard time breaking away from the computer, even for proper meals, there are programs available to download from the Internet that will provide an audible alarm to remind you it is time to get up and move around.

Taking regular breaks helps clear your mind, rest your eyes, gives your back, neck, shoulder and wrist muscles time to relax and overall is an easy way to get revitalized.

Communication   4

Companies must establish the priority of communication that remote workers will use to stay in touch with their supervisors. The priority will be determined by which method is easiest and most convenient for the remote worker to have access to. Within each company, the priority may vary according to the type of information or reporting to be done.

Here is a brief run down of the types of communication that are available and the order that should be used for communication between remote workers and their management.

Types of communication

Face to face

This is the preferred method as there is less likelihood of misinterpreting tone of voice or body language. It is not always possible, but regular face-to-face meetings should be scheduled between all remote workers and their supervisors. Face-to-face meetings provide an opportunity for remote workers and their supervisors to discuss work and other issues in a more relaxed, less formal and friendlier environment than solely relying on email or chat programs. Sometimes even a short meeting can be beneficial as it provides the time to get back in touch with those on site.

These meetings can be monthly or bi-weekly depending on the type of work or level of experience of the remote worker. Face-to-face meetings provide the opportunity for both sides to share news and keep each other up to date on developments, company news and any concerns that the remote worker or the supervisor may have.

Telephone (landlines/mobile phones/VoIP)

The use of the phone is the next best method, as it still allows for immediate feedback and response between the remote worker and the supervisor. It is useful as tone of voice can be read and explanations can be detailed and be clearly understood by both parties.

The downside to telephone calls is that they can be expensive if long distance calls are frequently made and time differences can limit availability. The remote worker may not always be in the same time zone as the person they are calling, therefore if information needs to shared immediately, time differences can prevent that. Another problem is that of missed telephone calls, which can become a game of 'telephone tag' where messages are left back and forth while the two parties are trying to reach other.

A last concern, which may be overlooked, is that for the remote worker there could be a great deal of background noise, which can interfere with how well a conversation is heard and understood.

4. COMMUNICATION

Phone calls can be made using traditional landline-based phone systems, mobile phones or over the Internet using Voice over Internet Protocol (VoIP). It is rare for any remote worker not to have a mobile phone and these can be much more convenient than landline phones as they can be used from most locations. With company-owned mobile phones, the company often selects the service plan, which may not always suit the needs of the remote workers. Companies should discuss with remote workers what types of service plans best suit their needs and the coverage they will require.

No matter who is responsible for purchasing the mobile phone and service plans, companies and remote workers should be clear on expectations of usage and who is responsible for paying for them. Security is another concern that will be addressed in more detail in a later chapter.

VoIP is still growing in popularity and can be even more beneficial to remote workers as they may be in a location that does not have a strong mobile phone signal, but where Internet access is available. Using a VoIP service does require downloading a small program or carrying an adapter.

Email

Email is convenient, and can be accessed from a variety of mobile devices, which makes it a preferred method for many remote workers. The major downside is that the tone of an email can easily be misinterpreted and short, quick messages can often omit important information.

Companies will need to establish guidelines as to proper use of email and this can include not using company email for personal use. The specific programs selected may be decided at a corporate level, or remote workers may be able to choose their own program to use. When selecting a program remote workers should determine what their needs are and what they want to be able to accomplish with their email program. Is a program that lets you send and receive messages only, such as Netscape, acceptable or do you need a more robust program such as Outlook, which includes more advanced features such as notes and calendar?

If remote workers will also be working from their home office and using that to store and keep track of emails then they should be sure that they have selected the option to leave email on the server when setting up their respective email program on their mobile equipment. This way they can check email while on the road but still have access to it once they are in their home office and using their desktop computer if applicable. Another option is using a web-based email system, which allows a remote worker to read and reply to email from any location, but they do not have to download the emails to their mobile equipment. This is useful because it ensures that in the event the mobile equipment is lost or stolen, there are no emails available to prying eyes and the risk of losing confidential data is lowered.

4. COMMUNICATION

When setting up email addresses, remote workers should remember to avoid using unprofessional names, which reflect poorly on them and their company. It can be tempting to create an email address that is unique and is funny, but these should be saved for personal email accounts.

The easy convenience of email is what also makes it a time eater. Remote workers should take care that they don't let their email control them throughout the workday. Set specific times for checking and replying to email and only check at those times. It is so easy to be overwhelmed and caught up in checking email that it becomes a distraction to getting any work done.

Additional guidelines regarding email use that a company may wish to implement are that slang should be avoided and that remote workers should be reminded to check and double-check that any email they are going to send is professional in tone and content.

Conferencing

There are options and programs available for both video and telephone conferencing that can be used to keep remote workers in touch with their co-workers and supervisors.

A telephone conference may be as simple as using the three-way calling feature on your mobile phone to a full blown company-wide conference call. Company-wide or departmental conference calls are normally handled through a third-party company. The calls are recorded and there are certain procedures to how the calls are conducted. Normally the person responsible for setting up the call will speak first and then allow for a question and answer period, during which anyone with a question is put into a queue and questions are answered in the order that the person was queued. This style of telephone conference is the most orderly and easiest to follow for participants.

A video conference can be a viable substitute to a face-to-face meeting when that is not possible due to cost or distance. Video conferencing requires that remote workers have high-speed Internet access, a microphone and a quality web camera. In many instances, the use of the Internet has made video conferencing easier and more economical to use than traditional phone conferences. Using video conferencing, remote workers and their on-site counterparts can share access to programs and images.

Companies may subscribe to a video conference service and have regularly scheduled conferences that remote workers can participate in when they are available and have reliable Internet access.

Prior to participating in a video conference, remote workers should connect and test their web cameras to ensure that they are able to use their mobile equipment properly and will be able to transmit a clear image and receive a good signal. Testing the audio send and receive should also be done before the actual video conference begins.

Care should be taken when scheduling conferences that any time differences are taken into consideration and that all participants can attend at the time scheduled.

Instant messaging

Instant messaging is another convenient way to share information and can be used with a variety of mobile devices such as personal digital assistants (PDAs), laptops and mobile phones. As with any other form of communication, it is important to remember that remote workers and their on-site counterparts should remain professional at all times and that the messages sent back and forth should not be shared with those outside the company. Care should also be taken that messaging is not used to avoid face-to-face meetings or phone calls. Quick updates or questions that are time sensitive are good reasons to use instant messaging.

Using the Internet

Internet

Everyone is familiar with what the Internet is and how it enables communication around the world and access to a wide variety of data and resources. The Internet has opened up new ways of doing business on both local and global levels. The Internet can be a valuable tool when used safely and wisely.

Intranets

Intranets are smaller network connections, which are used specifically by companies to allow information sharing between the corporate office and employees. Intranets can be used for easy access to corporate information that makes it easier for remote workers to work from any location. No longer do they have to carry huge manuals or sales brochures. These resources can be made available on a corporate intranet.

Most companies will take advantage of using a combination of the Internet and Intranet to enable their remote workers to stay connected and have access to resources while travelling. Relying only on one method can leave a remote worker in a position where they may not be able to connect or gain access to resources. If a corporate intranet is not possible, a company may choose to include the same type of information and resources on an Internet website, which is password protected and accessible only by employees.

Internet use policies

It is important for companies to develop and implement Internet use policies for all employees, including those who work remotely. This protects the company from any employee using the Internet in an unwise fashion and possibly opening the company up to litigation. If a company does not have an Internet use policy in place because they are still in the process of creating it, all employees should be given copies as soon as possible. All new employees should sign the Internet use policy as part of their first day paperwork.

Internet use policies must be signed by the employee and a company representative and held on file. Companies will have to determine what consequences an employee will face for failing to abide with the policy and ensure that those consequences are made clear in the Internet use policy, that the employee is made aware of them and that they are enforced. It is important that Internet use policies are reviewed on a regular basis and that changes in the availability of content on the Internet are taken into consideration for amendments.

An Internet use policy should cover the following:

5. USING THE INTERNET

- What uses are acceptable and when the Internet can be used.
- What uses are not allowed and the consequences of those uses.

Specific clauses should cover the following points, which should be tailored for each company.

- Acceptable use of the Internet for completing job-related tasks such as research or email. Forwarding jokes and chain letter-type emails should be expressly forbidden.
- When the Internet may be used for personal use.
- Specify the Internet resources available and for which employees these resources are available – this can include services such as uploading or downloading files. If all employees use these then it is possible to cause an overload or cause this service to be unavailable at a critical time for remote workers.
- Internet activities that are not permitted should be listed individually so that it is clear what is not allowed. These can include accessing online gambling websites, pornographic websites and sites that provide downloads of programs or multimedia content.
- Specify that firewall and anti-virus software must be installed and kept updated.

If a company decides to employ monitoring equipment, this should be stated in the Internet use policy so that employees can never claim that they were not aware that they were being monitored. In circumstances where remote workers are using their own mobile equipment, different factors will need to be taken into consideration. Monitoring equipment cannot be installed without the consent of the remote worker and their use of the Internet cannot be dictated. The company can create a safe use policy for remote workers.

This safe use policy should include clauses that state that remote workers should demonstrate care and caution while using the Internet in order to protect the corporate network and data contained on their mobile equipment. Many remote workers do not realize that they can put their own mobile equipment and the resources of the company at great risk by careless use of the Internet.

- All remote workers should be encouraged to visit only safe websites (safe websites are those that the company has approved such as the corporate website and Intranet if one exists, client sites and supplier sites) and to avoid downloading programs or multimedia from sites they are not familiar with.
- Firewall and anti-virus software are installed to improve and provide protection.
- To provide more protection to the corporate resources, remote workers should consider using web-filtering software.
- When possible, encryption software should be used for email and file storage.

Companies that do not create Internet use and safe use policies leave themselves open to the potential of very costly lawsuits and loss of revenue. All remote workers must be made aware of how their own actions can adversely affect their employer and cause repercussions from which they may not recover.

Preventing problems

The first step to preventing problems with Internet access is to provide clear Internet use and/or safe use policies and to ensure that signed copies of these are placed on file for all remote workers. Once this has been done, it is next up to the company to provide resources for the remote workers to learn more about the potential risks they face while working remotely and what solutions the company will provide.

Potential risks include:

- using a computer in a hot spot without having first installed firewall and anti-virus software;
- using public computers such as those found in Internet cafes and accessing confidential data without a means to prevent others from gaining access to that data once you have left;
- potential hackers gaining access to mobile gear through the use of unsafe websites and unprotected wireless Internet connections;
- theft – this is the leading cause of lost and compromised data that companies face.

Chapter 7 takes a more detailed look at security and how companies and their remote workers can protect their data and mobile gear.

Companies should take time to provide training sessions so that remote workers can learn more about protecting their data while on the road. There are many companies that provide seminars to explain how to identify and avoid risks, which is beneficial for all employees to know.

When companies pay for and/or provide Internet access for their remote workforce it should be noted in any policy that the Internet service is provided first as a means for a remote worker to fulfill the tasks of their position and make it easier to communicate while working remotely. Internet access is not provided for recreational purposes for the remote worker.

Companies may be able to control when remote workers access the Internet by having service plans in place that restrict the time and availability of Internet access.

Remote workers should be careful and use the Internet wisely and safely, or they may take the attitude that, if no one can see what they are doing, they can surf whichever websites they want and download anything they want.

Remote workers who adopt the latter approach are more likely to cause problems and put their companies at an increased risk of harm. It is important that all remote workers understand that in order to continue to work in a remote capacity they take seriously how they use the Internet and the potential impact it can have on the rest of the company.

5. USING THE INTERNET

In Chapter 7, we look more closely at security for remote workers and how they can be taught to protect their data and their mobile equipment while working remotely.

Making connections 6

Now that we have discussed safe Internet use, it is time to look at methods of accessing the Internet and other connections that are possible. Remote workers will need the ability to connect their mobile equipment to each other in order to share and transfer information as well as connect to the Internet. There is a variety of options for both and in many cases these connections can be used for both purposes.

Decide which connection you need

Companies should not rely on only one method of connection for their remote workers.

Although budgetary considerations will be the determining factor when a company reviews which type of Internet access to provide to their remote workers, it is far better to have more than one type of connection so that there is a back up available for when other methods fail or are not available.

While many people are glad to move from dial-up access to faster methods such as broadband services, having a dial-up account available can be a lifesaver.

Computer-to-computer

This is the smallest type of network connection and can be as simple as a cable between your laptop and a desktop to share files and peripherals. When you need to access another computer on an occasional basis, this is a good solution.

Bluetooth™ [1]

This is another option that is useful for sharing information between a PDA or mobile phone and your laptop (or vice versa) and between your laptop and printers, or equally between laptops. One nice advantage to Bluetooth™ is that you do not need to have both gadgets lined up with each other.

Bluetooth™ is quite easy to set up and use. Even if remote workers have older desktop systems or laptops that they use, it is easy to purchase a Bluetooth™ dongle that connects to an available USB port to add Bluetooth™ capabilities.

It should be noted that some mobile phones and smart phones have had their Bluetooth™ capability disabled by the service provider. If Bluetooth™ is important to the way that your remote workers will work, make sure that the phone they will use is Bluetooth™ enabled.

---

[1]The Bluetooth™ trademark is owned by the Bluetooth SIG, Inc. This information is given for the convenience of users of this book and does not constitute an endorsement by BSI of the technology named.

6. MAKING CONNECTIONS

A Bluetooth™ connection between a laptop and mobile phone can be used as a way to connect to the Internet. By creating a connection between the two, the cell phone can be used as a modem (make sure that the remote workers have data service plans on their phones first) and this can be a good alternative when other Internet access services are not available.

Remote workers should not leave their Bluetooth™ turned on, as it will drain the battery of mobile equipment, even when not in use and there is the risk that someone else with a Bluetooth™ device will connect and attempt to access data.

Infrared

Infrared is another type of networking connection that uses light waves to connect to PDAs, mobile phones, printers and other computers. For infrared to be successful you have to ensure that both devices are in line with each other and close together. Even moving one gadget the slightest amount can break the connection.

Dial-up Internet access

Dial-up networking can be used to connect to the Internet, another computer or a corporate network. Dial-up is a slow connection and not useful if you have large amounts of data to share or transfer. In some areas, dial-up connection is still the only option available to get access to the Internet.

Although dial-up is a slower connection method it can be a more economical choice when other more expensive methods such as satellite are the only alternative. An advantage to dial-up access is that most Internet Service Providers (ISPs) will have local access numbers for the area that they cover – in some cases countrywide.

Remote workers should be provided with all the access numbers from their ISP for the locations they will be travelling to. Once a laptop has been set up for dial-up access, it is easy to go in and switch the access number for the location being worked at.

In order to use dial-up access a laptop will need a modem, which are integrated for many laptop models. An external modem will need to be purchased if the laptop does not have one.

Issues with dial-up not working properly are normally due to faulty or old telephone lines being used. All remote workers should therefore carry their own RJ-11 telephone line to use to connect to wall jacks.

Broadband/Ethernet

Cable and DSL (digital subscriber line) are both types of broadband access. Transfer times are faster than dial-up and you can share Internet connections with the help of routers and switches.

Broadband networks use Ethernet cables to create connections between computers, the Internet and gadgets. Broadband can now be used in more locations as many companies offer plug-in modems that can use any phone line to connect to your broadband account. Broadband networks can be at the whim of the service provider and may not always be 100% reliable. Weather and quality of phone lines and cable lines can affect performance.

An interesting new twist for broadband that is offered by both cable and DSL companies is the 'broadband anywhere' concept. A portable router that connects to an electrical outlet is used wherever the broadband company provides service and the remote worker will be able to have high-speed Internet access wherever they are working.

Wireless networking (Wi-Fi)

Wi-Fi (wireless fidelity) networking is a set of standards that have been based on the specifications known as IEEE 802.11. The original design was to enable users to connect devices without wires but it is possible to use Wi-Fi to connect to the Internet without wires.

Wi-Fi networking opens the most possibilities. It is what enables you to use hot spots, eliminate wires, and connect to additional mobile equipment and share resources. Wireless networks can be combined with broadband networks to expand the possibilities for connecting mobile equipment.

Remote workers can research before leaving the office on business trips to map out where Wi-Fi locations are during their travels or a Wi-Fi detector can be purchased. This small gadget is used to locate and identify Wi-Fi signals. Using a Wi-Fi detector means you do not have to keep turning on your laptop or other wireless equipment just to check for signals.

Wi-Fi is a great convenience for remote workers but security must be stressed to all who use it. Malicious users can gain access to data on equipment using Wi-Fi. These attacks can take the form of WiPhishing or what is called the 'evil twin threat'. WiPhishing occurs when a hacker creates an illegal access point and uses a valid SSID (service set identifier) to trick remote workers into accessing the illegal access point. Once a remote worker enters an illegal access point, their mobile equipment becomes vulnerable to the hacker who can access their data. The evil twin threat method involves redirecting a remote worker to an illegal access point created by the hacker. While both these methods may appear extreme and highly unlikely, they are possible and a definite threat to the safety of data contained on a remote worker's mobile equipment. Wi-Fi should only be turned on when needed, to reduce the risk of someone trying to access the wireless-enabled device and to avoid draining the battery.

Virtual private networks (VPNs)

VPNs are a direct connection to a corporate system. Companies can let remote workers use the VPN to access corporate data such as client lists, company training resources and schedule information. Using this method of access eliminates the need for the remote workers to keep this information on their own mobile equipment.

File transfer protocol (FTP)

While not traditionally considered a networking option, using FTP can be an inexpensive and useful option for remote workers. Companies can set up FTP access for employees to download information and resources, upload files for others to access and download shared work. FTP is handy because you can use a stand-alone FTP program or your web browser to move files around. You can also use FTP from any location and it saves storing files on your mobile equipment on a permanent basis. It is recommended that companies change the FTP password on a scheduled basis to help prevent unauthorized access.

Mobile phones

Many mobile phones can be used as a modem for other Internet-enabled mobile equipment. It should be noted that it is a wise idea to have a data service plan on the mobile phone. Even though some service providers will allow a mobile phone to be used as a modem and will only charge against minutes used, there are companies that charge for data uploads and downloads and this can become a very expensive method to use.

Evolution data only/Evolution data optimized (EVDO)

EVDO (also known as 1xEvDO, EV-DO or EvDO) is a method of accessing the Internet using mobile phone signals. It is like cable and DSL access in that it is always on and available when needed. While it is not widely available, that is changing. Using EVDO, a remote worker can access the Internet from their vehicle, a train, hotels and other locations.

In order to use EVDO, a remote worker needs an EVDO card to access the signals and enable their mobile equipment to access the Internet.

Worldwide Interoperability for Microwave Access (WiMax)

WiMax is another emerging technology that will allow remote workers to connect to the Internet from a greater variety of locations.

In a similar way to Wi-Fi, no cables, routers or modems are needed to be connected to a laptop or other wireless-enabled mobile equipment. WiMax is a long-range system as opposed to the short signals that Wi-Fi generates.

Code division multiple access (CDMA2000)

Code division multiple access is a combination of 2G and 3G used for sending voice, data and signal data between cell phones and cell sites.

CDMA is also known as CDMA 1xRTT, CDMA2000 EV-DO or CDMA20000 EV-DV. It provides increased speed for cell phone signals and the ability to upload/download data.

Universal mobile telecommunications system (UMTS)

Universal mobile telecommunications system is a mobile phone technology commonly referred to as a third-generation (3G) technology. UMTS is often referred to as 3GSM.

It is used for mobile phone access and if the phone is capable then it can be used a modem to connect a laptop to the Internet.

Satellite

Satellite connections are the most expensive form of connection and usually reserved for remote workers who have no other option available. Signals are sent and received via communication satellites, which are owned by a variety of companies. One of the interesting aspects of satellite connections and something that companies should be aware of is that not all satellite access connections allow for two-way traffic. What this means is that the satellite access may only allow for information to be downloaded – such as email or viewing websites but a user cannot upload or send email.

Satellite is still only available for Internet access to stationary locations, you can't be driving in a vehicle and use satellite access to connect to the Internet. There are also issues with interference with satellite signals, which can make it less than reliable and an option of last resort. Both cable and DSL connections are more economical, easier to set up and use and more reliable.

Security

Why be concerned?

Security is extremely important and should be of the utmost concern to all parties involved with remote work. Laptops and other mobile gear are expensive investments and it is important to take all steps within your control to keep them protected, working properly and ensuring that the information they contain stays safe.

Every company will have the same basic security needs and, in addition, they may have their own specific situations that will require different security solutions.

Data that has been compromised through unsafe work habits or negligent security guidelines can create huge expenses that a company may not fully recover from.

We've all heard the news stories about laptops and portable storage drives being stolen that contained confidential information. Don't let that be your company.

Most countries now have data protection legislation in place that dictates how a company can use confidential information, who is allowed access and how that information is to be stored, protected and even for how long the information may be kept. It is important to note that one of the most common clauses in data protection legislation in different countries states that data may only be transferred to other countries that offer similar or adequate data protection.

Companies are responsible for exercising due care and diligence when dealing with data that is covered by this legislation. Burning a CD or DVD with all their client details is probably not a wise idea, nor is putting all this information on a portable drive, which can be easily lost or stolen.

The best way for companies to keep this type of information properly protected is to keep it on a central server and with proper safety precautions in place allow remote workers to have access to this central data collection.

Safe use policies for mobile equipment

Safe use policies govern how remote employees may use company-provided mobile equipment while travelling, how they may use the Internet from that equipment and detail how to work safely when travelling to protect their mobile equipment and the data that it contains.

For laptops in particular, using the Internet and sending and receiving email can be risky if you fail to provide protection against potential dangers. If you have not protected your laptop properly, you may fall prey to some nasty creations courtesy of the Internet. Malware, including viruses, can wreak havoc both on information stored in computer systems and on communications systems. Worms and bugs take on whole new meanings for unprotected laptops.

7. SECURITY

Companies should not have blanket safe use policies for all employees, but should tailor their policies to reflect specific positions and types of mobile equipment that are involved. Safe use policies should include when mobile equipment can be used and when it should not be used, such as not using mobile phones without a hands-free kit while operating a motor vehicle, unless already prohibited by law.

Laptop safety

The purpose of using a variety of methods to protect your laptop is to make it a less desirable target to thieves. Keeping your laptop in a secure case, using laptop locks and password protection will all combine to make things more complicated and time-consuming for a thief.

Passwords

Most new laptops have built-in security features that, when used properly, can help protect the data they contain. Passwords should be changed on a regular basis and a record kept of which passwords have been used. Don't keep this record on the laptop. A simple notebook or file card system is adequate, if you need to keep track of the passwords that you have chosen. Don't keep this record with you while travelling.

When creating passwords (this applies not only to BIOS passwords – see below), there are certain words that should be avoided. These include, but are not limited to:

- the user's name;
- phone numbers;
- the term 'admin' should not be used (you may find it is the default password for some mobile equipment);
- 123, 1234 or other sequential number combinations;
- money;
- easily guessed phrases, like 'opensesame', or 'letmein', etc.;
- real words taken from dictionaries.

Good passwords are those that use both alpha and numeric combinations such as:

- 3goodword4;
- dandy4me;
- krow9317;
- packer5315;
- safet1st4u.

As you can see by the example passwords (which are more complex), they do not reflect anything personal about the user and there are letters and numbers mixed within the password. Nonsense words combined with numbers are much harder to crack as there is no rhyme or reason to them. Make your password as illogical as possible.

BIOS

BIOS stands for Basic Input/Output System. Think of the BIOS in your laptop as the brain. The BIOS is the controller of all hardware and

7. SECURITY

software in your computer system, whether it is a laptop or a desktop. The BIOS passes on the commands from the operating system and other programs to the hardware. The BIOS can be stored in the ROM or stored on a Flash memory chip of the motherboard.

This protection begins at the BIOS level and users can enable a password to prevent system booting or from changes being made to the BIOS. Not all laptops will use the same methods for setting the BIOS password and the user guide should be consulted in order to ensure that the password has been set correctly.

Operating system

Setting a password at the operating system level is adding another level of security to a laptop. This can also be useful if laptops are used by different users. Each can have their own password to login to the laptop for access to their files.

Screen saver

If remote workers may be away from their laptop – even for a couple minutes in an otherwise secure environment – but don't wish to shut down completely they can enable the screen saver password option. This means that the screen saver will be activated after a set time and in order to get back into the laptop a password must be entered.

Third-party programs

Third-party programs can be installed to add password protection to a laptop. Since most operating systems have built-in password protection capabilities, this type of program may not be required.

While there are some who may scoff at using this many passwords on their laptop or consider it to be too much hassle, it really isn't and using a minimum of two levels of password protection is advised. Passwords should never be stored on the laptop, whether for websites or access to networks. Don't enable the password to be saved, that just makes it easier for someone to gain access if your laptop is stolen.

While having strong password protection may not deter a thief from taking your laptop if you have been identified as an easy target, it can prevent them gaining access to the information it contains. Granted, this may mean your laptop will end up in a rubbish bin, pawn shop or with the hard drive removed and sold 'as is'.

Additional methods of protecting your laptop are detailed further in this chapter and it is the combination of using all possible methods that will keep your laptop and the data it contains safe.

Biometrics

Biometrics are the means of using measurable physical characteristics such as fingerprints or palm prints (fingerprints for laptops) to verify the identity of authorized users. There are more advanced biometric systems, which utilize voice recognition or facial recognition, but these are not yet parts of laptop security enhancements.

Biometrics are a very useful means of protecting laptop computers as it is very difficult to copy someone's fingerprint. There are laptop models that have integrated fingerprint sensors, and there are also stand-alone fingerprint readers, which connect to the laptop via USB.

If a company is updating their laptops, then selecting a model with an integrated biometric fingerprint reader is a good idea. If they aren't going to be updating their laptops in the near future, then purchasing external fingerprint sensors is a wise investment.

It is important to let remote workers know that just because they now have use of fingerprint sensors they should not get lax in their use of passwords. Using both passwords and fingerprint sensors is best.

Having secured laptops with passwords and biometrics it is time to consider some other external methods of protecting them.

Notebook security cables

Notebook security cables can be used while visiting client offices or working in hotel rooms to secure a laptop to a non-moveable surface. The cables can also be used within a laptop case to keep the laptop secured to the inside of the laptop case. There are varieties of cable-locking systems available – some have keyed locks and others have combination locks.

Privacy filters

Using a privacy filter while travelling helps keep prying eyes from viewing your laptop display. Privacy filters are not expensive and work well. They are especially useful during airline flights or while waiting in airports.

Laptop bags

A secure laptop bag will provide some protection against theft, as well as against damage from knocks and from weather conditions. Companies should not purchase laptop bags and get them emblazoned with their company name or logo as this just serves to create a more tempting target. Look for laptop bags that are well constructed, have sturdy zippers, have a weather resistant exterior and room for accessories inside. Laptop backpacks and bags that have both carry handles and shoulder straps are the most versatile styles of laptop bags. There are some hybrid versions that can be used as either a backpack or shoulder bag. These enable remote workers to keep their hands free while travelling if they use the laptop bag in backpack mode. When carrying a lighter load it can be used with the shoulder strap.

If remote workers are to purchase their own laptop bags, a company can set guidelines that will help remote workers select the best laptop bag to

7. SECURITY

suit their needs. These guidelines can include recommendations for brand, style and price. Companies should survey remote workers to see what details a laptop bag has that appeals to them and which laptop bags they have used in the past and why they liked or disliked a particular type.

When using a laptop bag, small locks should also be used to secure the laptop bag against someone attempting to remove the laptop. Most zippers have fastenings that make it possible to attach a small lock.

Alarms

Audible alarms are an effective deterrent to theft. These alarms can be attached to laptop bags and activate when the laptop bag is moved or when an attempt is made to open it.

Laptop tracking systems

Laptop tracking systems are a newer technology that is available, not only for laptops but also for other mobile equipment. One system involves installing a software program that runs silently in the background. This program is very hard to detect and, for the most part, thieves will not be aware of its presence.

Once a piece of mobile equipment has been reported lost or stolen, the software is activated to send a message or alert to a reporting centre when the mobile equipment is used to access the Internet. The software then tracks the location of the mobile equipment and law enforcement personnel can be contacted. There are options available with some tracking systems to allow for remotely deleting files and storing them on a web-based server so that the information can be protected and transferred safely.

Data encryption

This is a method to protect the contents of your mobile equipment from unauthorized users. Using a software program, data is encrypted and only by entering a code or password can the data be accessed and decrypted. If an unauthorized user gains access to the remote worker's mobile equipment, he or she will only be able to view what appears to be gibberish and nonsensical information.

Remote workers should be trained and encouraged to encrypt their data files to provide an additional level of protection.

Firewalls and anti-virus programs

When a company or a remote worker purchases any mobile equipment, it is important that before the equipment is used it is set up correctly for optimum safety. This means that a firewall program and anti-virus software should be installed.

Firewall programs learn how you use programs, and browse the Internet to know what programs users should be allowed access to, such as program updates, and provide alerts when there is activity that is not

7. SECURITY

expected – typically a program that is attempting to connect to the Internet or a connection coming from the Internet. Malicious programs that may have been hidden within other programs and installed at the same time are noted for this type of activity. The firewall program selected should protect from both inbound (attacks coming from the Internet) and outbound communications (your computer trying to communicate with someone or something).

An anti-virus program should be installed after the firewall is installed. This will protect not only the individual laptop but also others that share a network connection or those to and from which files are transferred.

Both of these programs together help protect a laptop from attempts to gain access either through the Internet or wireless connections. Prior to any remote worker going out on their first trip or when receiving a new laptop, it should be verified that the laptop they will be using has had these software programs installed, that they are up to date and will be running.

Remote workers must be told that deactivating the firewall or anti-virus software is not considered acceptable. In the safe use policy mentioned in Chapter 5, there should be a clause that details the importance of using these programs and keeping them up to date, and what the consequences of failing to do so are.

It should also be pointed out that when remote workers use their laptops for work purposes that even if they only have dial-up Internet access, they still should have firewall and anti-virus programs running.

Firewalls and anti-virus programs don't need to be expensive to be the best solution either. There are free versions of both programs available that work very well, are reliable and are not difficult to find either. The only downside is that the initial pop-up screens that notify you a program is accessing the Internet may be mildly annoying. Once you approve the programs as necessary, you won't see those again unless something new is trying to access the Internet. When you see the pop-up screen and it notifies you of a program that is not known to you, don't allow it to access the Internet until you can investigate and learn more about the program.

It is advantageous for companies to purchase one type of program for firewall protection and anti-virus protection for all remote workers, rather than having a wide variety of programs running and trying to troubleshoot and provide support for different programs.

Spyware protection

Installing spyware protection software is another way to protect your laptop. Spyware is another nasty creature of the Internet. It is another form of software that has been created with less than honourable intentions. Spyware can make changes to your system, gather personal information and blast pop-up advertising. You don't even have to be online for these nasty surprises to occur. Once your laptop is infected, additional changes by these programs may occur and it can be very difficult to change back to your original settings. There are free programs available that are effective in removing spyware and preventing it from infiltrating computer systems.

PDA and mobile phone safety

Most remote workers don't spend much time worrying about the safety of their PDA or mobile phones yet these mobile devices can and should be password protected. Use the same method of creating and changing passwords on a PDA or mobile phone as would be used on a laptop. There are some models of PDA that have integrated fingerprint sensors. Encrypting the data on a PDA is probably more important than encrypting the data on a laptop, as a PDA can be easier to misplace or to steal.

External storage cards used with PDAs and/or mobile phones should be kept secure and not with the PDA when not in use. Although many PDA and mobile phone cases provide storage for these external cards it is wiser to get another secure case just for storage cards and keep it separate from the device. If a large enough storage card is used, then all data can be stored on the card and if the PDA or mobile phone is lost or stolen no important data is lost.

Owner information

When setting up a PDA or mobile phone for the first time, the owner information is requested. You do not have to enter anything at this point and you will not be prompted at intervals to enter this later. Entering the information can be useful if a co-worker finds the device and doesn't know who it belongs to because the information can be used to track down the owner. However, keeping a record of serial and model numbers is adequate in case of loss for reporting purposes. Also, confidential information such as an address or phone number could end up in the wrong hands. Once a mobile gadget has been stolen, the thief is likely to change the owner information.

Companies that provide PDAs or mobile phones to their employees may enter owner information using only company details, such as company name and a unique identifier, which may be the method they use to track mobile gear. While this appears to be a sound idea, it does provide additional incentive to an unauthorized user to make use of any information that is available from the device such as contact information and other data for illegal or malicious intentions.

Travel security

Overview

While travelling, especially to other countries, it is important that remote workers are properly prepared. Keeping a laptop bag tidy, with the right paperwork prepared and readily accessible, rather than overfilling it with unnecessary paperwork or files will make dealing with both Customs and security checkpoints a smoother process for all involved. Remember to learn the rules of what is required to enter another country or return to the country of origin so that no problems will arise and trips will not be delayed.

Don't leave for trips at the last minute but leave with enough time to get through security and Customs. Ensure that laptops are removed from laptop cases and make sure that the battery is charged so that if requested it can be started.

Companies should provide all remote workers with lists of what items are not allowed on flights – both domestic and international – so that remote workers can pack properly.

Customs

When dealing with Customs it is important to remember that remote workers must provide proof of ownership of all mobile equipment and be ready to show what equipment they have in their laptop bag. An inventory list can be created, which includes model and serial numbers for all mobile equipment, and presented to the Customs official, which can speed up the process and make getting cleared much easier.

Remote workers who purchase additional mobile equipment will need to provide receipts that show where the device was purchased as there may be duties and taxes imposed for the purchase.

Checkpoints

Security checkpoints are now a common feature in most airports and even in some rail stations. Checkpoints are generally found when travelling between countries and they are there to ensure the safety and security of all passengers. Remote workers should keep in mind that they are not being picked on or targeted. Approach any security checkpoints with a pleasant disposition and willingness to answer questions and have mobile equipment inspected.

All the right gear

8

Best equipment for the job

Once a company has arrived at the decision to create remote work programmes, they must then decide what type of mobile equipment is to be used by the remote workers. Companies will need to determine whether they will purchase the mobile equipment for their workers, if remote workers will purchase their own mobile equipment and be reimbursed for this, or whether the remote workers will purchase the mobile equipment with no reimbursement.

If a company decides to go the route of purchasing the mobile equipment themselves, they will need to consider the following.

- What is the budget for all equipment required?
- What are the job functions of all potential remote workers?
- Will mobile devices be purchased outright or leased?
- Are the potential purchases compatible with existing equipment?
- Which mobile devices are best suited to each worker's responsibilities?

Budget considerations

When a company is considering their budget for mobile equipment they need to determine what type of mobile equipment will be purchased or leased, how much the software costs will be and what type of additional accessories may be required for remote workers to work productively and securely while on the road.

Time should be spent researching different options such as:

- what different manufacturers offer in terms of warranty and service;
- what type of deals may be available for things like large quantity purchases;
- what type of upgrade features are available;
- leasing options and lease terms;
- what type of training (if any) or help service is available.

Review job functions

At the same time that the budget considerations are being evaluated, the review of job functions should be completed.

Factors to be taken into consideration here include the following.

- Will remote workers need to create documents, presentations or graphic art designs?
- Will information need to be shared with co-workers and customers?
- How often will Internet access or corporate network access be required?
- Will remote workers need to print (black and white or colour)?
- Is file transfer capability required?

8. ALL THE RIGHT GEAR

- What type of files would need to be saved?
- Is the ability to use web or video conferencing a priority?
- What resources would need to be readily accessible on a mobile device? These resources could include:
  - price manuals for your company and competitors, if available;
  - legal references such as by-laws or citations;
  - building codes;
  - image libraries, which include sample layouts for interior designers, etc.

An easy way to determine the above is to select one or two positions that meet the criteria for remote work consideration and then have the appropriate employee monitor their workflow and work habits for a two-week period. Selecting two different jobs should provide companies with enough data to evaluate what mobile equipment will be required for remote workers to be productive and what specific equipment and models will meet those needs.

Purchase or lease?

Companies will make this decision after resolving their budget considerations as they will then know how much money they have available. Leasing mobile equipment can be advantageous in some situations, though it can be a double-edged sword – you may be able to have lease terms customized so that upgrades of equipment are possible to allow for

77

new technologies, or the lease term may be iron-clad and you will not be able to upgrade until the current term ends.

Compatibility with existing equipment

It makes no sense to buy mobile equipment that cannot be used with existing equipment that a company already owns. Compatibility issues include the ability to use wireless connections to synchronize data between devices and the types of ports on equipment. The ability for devices – both mobile and fixed – to 'talk' with each other using direct cable or wireless connections such as infrared should be borne in mind when purchasing new equipment.

Providing remote workers with a mobile phone, PDA or laptop enabled to transmit information to another mobile device is pointless if this device is an older model that does not have those capabilities.

It is possible to upgrade and provide some wireless technologies to an existing computer but it should be determined first whether the company or the individual will be responsible for this type of equipment upgrade.

Types of mobile equipment

Converged devices/smartphones

Converged devices have made an impact on how work can be done in a remote environment.

8. ALL THE RIGHT GEAR

A converged device that combines the features of multiple devices (e.g. PDA, laptop and mobile phone) enables a remote worker to carry fewer items and worry less about losing a device. On the downside, having just one device to rely on for all communications needs, data storage and means of work can be dangerous. If the device fails, the remote worker can lose all data necessary for carrying out their job and the means by which to work and contact others.

Converged devices can work well for executives who are not responsible for creating new documentation yet need a way to view data and stay in touch while away from the office.

Laptops

Laptops are available in a variety of styles and dimensions. To determine which will best suit the needs of your remote workforce, a clear understanding of what tasks they will be performing is required. This goes back to the process of reviewing job functions mentioned earlier in this chapter.

The time remote workers spend getting used to a particular type of laptop can have an impact on their productivity. If using a laptop that is not one they are used to, time should be made available for training.

It is strongly recommended that for any laptop purchases, an extra battery is always included. This can be crucial for a remote worker when there is no other power source available.

Depending on the nature of work performed, it is not always necessary to get a laptop that has all the latest features. For example, having a large display makes it easier to view documents and websites, but it is not essential for all remote workers. Money can be saved by choosing models that have smaller displays.

Important features to look for in laptops for remote workers include:

- a wide variety of Internet connection options (Wi-Fi, Ethernet, internal modem);
- a comfortable keyboard;
- I/O ports that enable a remote worker to use additional peripherals;
- an external monitor port;
- a parallel printer port.

Rugged laptops

Rugged laptops, as their name implies, are stronger and more durable than their standard-built counterparts. Not everyone will need a rugged laptop but learning more about what they are and what they offer may prove useful to you in the future.

The military and outdoor industries such as construction and utility companies are more likely to purchase rugged laptops than the ordinary consumer.

Rugged laptops have been designed to handle the following:

8. ALL THE RIGHT GEAR

- extreme temperatures;
- vibrations (more intense than being carried in a vehicle);
- dust getting into components;
- liquid spills;
- drops and shock.

Rugged laptops are rated according to how well they will handle different circumstances such as being dropped, what weather extremes they will operate under and how well they prevent dirt and dust from getting inside.

Water resistance is measured by how much liquid (e.g. snow, rain, water in a boating environment or liquids other than water) the rugged laptop can be subjected to and still operate.

Shock resistance is measured by the highest height that a rugged laptop can be dropped from and still operate.

Vibration resistance is measured by the amount of continuous vibration a rugged laptop will handle while it is being used.

These specifications are measured and tested in labs before the laptop can be validated as meeting the manufacturer's specifications. The most common standard is the military MIL STD 810F. This standard was created by the American government and includes a wide set of tests that are used to judge the ruggedness of a laptop.

Another rating system is Ingress Protection or IP. The IP number is used to measure the environmental protection of the electronic equipment.

The letters IP are followed by two numbers. The first number indicates how well the equipment is protected from moving parts and the degree to which the internal components are protected from objects getting inside. The second number refers to protection against moisture entering the internal components.

The features of a rugged laptop will differ from conventional laptops:

- displays are designed to be used indoors and outdoors;
- backlit keyboards;
- hard disks are solid state disks (SSD), which have no mechanical moving parts;
- ports and connectors are sealed;
- spill proof keyboards that are sealed;
- no internal optical disk drives.

Rugged laptops have a distinctive appearance and are not as sleek or stylish as their non-rugged counterparts. They often have smaller displays and the casing is very military looking and bulky. Rugged laptops, even with smaller displays, can weigh more than a conventional laptop with the same display size.

Semi-rugged laptops

Semi-rugged laptops are becoming more common and even traditional laptop manufacturers are beginning to design them. These semi-rugged

8. ALL THE RIGHT GEAR

laptops are more expensive than their conventional counterparts but may offer more features, such as optical disk drives and port availability, than fully rugged laptops. They are also heavier, as the protective additions increase the overall weight. The casing in most instances is made completely from magnesium alloy.

Semi-rugged laptops are designed to withstand spills on the keyboard and damage to the hard drive. The hard drives have additional protection against being dropped.

Some models actually have something similar to a car airbag to protect the hard drive when it is dropped.

Why go rugged?

If you are seriously considering a rugged laptop, be aware of what you will and won't be getting for your money.

Rugged and semi-rugged laptops will put a serious dent in your wallet and, unless you can live without certain features, you are better off getting a non-rugged laptop and taking extra precautions when using it outdoors.

Rugged laptops work well in the outdoors and extreme weather because that is what they are designed for. The average person won't need these capabilities and the price of these models is normally the deciding factor.

Rugged and semi-rugged laptops may also lack some of the more commonly used ports and connections useful to remote workers. This is due to the fact that fewer openings mean that the equipment can be more easily protected from the environment. While some rugged and semi-rugged laptops do have removable port covers, these can be lost or damaged and thus increase the chance of dirt and other debris entering the laptop.

Companies and industries are more likely to buy rugged laptops for their corps of workers who need the convenience of laptop computing but require a much sturdier machine such as those in the construction, utility and law enforcement fields.

Tablet PCs

Tablet PCs are an alternative to laptops. They are smaller and can be useful especially if a remote worker is required to enter a lot of information quickly and easily.

There are three styles of tablet PC – slate, convertible and rugged tablet PC. Slate tablet PCs are just the display and do not have an integrated keyboard. This makes them more compact and easy to carry.

Convertible tablet PCs look like a regular laptop but the display can be turned to make it possible to enter information directly with a stylus (a digital pen that doesn't use ink but is used to control your actions and input information using handwriting or tapping menu commands) or

8. ALL THE RIGHT GEAR

the keyboard can be used. You don't even have to use the stylus that comes with your tablet PC; try to find one that is the most comfortable for you and has the right functions available. There are some types of tablet PC stylus available that include eraser tips and programmable buttons for right-click selections.

Rugged tablet PCs are more robust versions of convertible tablet PCs that are designed to be used out in the elements.

Tablet PCs are more expensive than traditional laptops, and a company would have to evaluate the benefits of using Tablet PCs over traditional laptops to determine whether the price difference is worth paying.

Ultra mobile (micro) personal computers (UMPCs)

The UMPC entered the market in 2006. It is an interesting device that takes the phrase 'portable computing' to a new dimension.

UMPCs have the computing capability of laptops but are the size of PDAs. They can run the same programs as would be used on a laptop. The processors and battery life are not as powerful as a laptop, so this may not be a suitable option if a remote worker needs to be able to run a number of programs at the same time.

The UMPC is not being touted as a replacement for laptops or PDAs but as another alternative. It is a tool for convenience and ease of use.

It is an expensive alternative to your laptop or PDA as the UMPCs currently available are rather costly for the added convenience they offer. Unless you have a real need to keep up with all portable technologies no matter what the cost, it would be better to wait until the UMPC has dropped in price and offers better features.

PDAs

PDAs are useful tools for inputting data and, if wireless enabled, they can be used to access the Internet. It is not recommended that remote workers rely on a PDA to do all their work, but rather use it for taking notes and organizing information for later transfer to a laptop.

PDAs vary in price range depending on the features that they contain. If used only as a method for quickly taking notes, keeping track of appointments and keeping research information organized then a PDA is a great addition to a remote worker's inventory of mobile equipment.

PDAs are quicker to access than laptops as they start immediately and access to programs can be quicker.

Which brand a company selects will be determined by which laptops they purchase and what operating system they use in the company office. If a company purchases PDAs for their remote workforce it would be a wise idea to ensure that all remote workers have the same model for the following reasons.

- Firstly, it is easier to ensure compatibility with other mobile and fixed equipment.
- Secondly, not all PDAs use the same operating system, and having a PDA that works with a different operating system than that currently used by a company could cause problems as additional software or hardware could be required to enable data sharing between the PDA and other mobile equipment.
- Thirdly, it makes troubleshooting easier if the company works with the same models for mobile equipment because there is one operating system and one model of equipment for the IT department to work with. It is much easier to learn the quirks of one versus a variety of different models of equipment and multiple operating systems.
- Last but not least, it can be better for the budget as it is easier to work out deals for large purchases of mobile equipment than a few here and there.

Mobile phones

When companies look at which mobile phone to acquire for their remote workers, the service plans should be evaluated first. If the mobile phone service provider does not have plans that are economical or offer features that are needed then it really doesn't matter how great the mobile phone may be.

Things to consider when choosing a mobile phone and provider include:

- whether there is unlimited calling between subscribers;
- whether there is international roaming;
- whether their customer services are easily contactable and helpful;
- whether there are plans that can be customized for different users.

It is worth discussing with service providers what types of deals they may be able to arrange for companies based on the number of mobile phones to be used and purchased.

Selecting a mobile phone can be a very personal decision for some people. They have very definite likes and dislikes with regard to style and how a mobile phone looks. Once a company has narrowed down which service provider they want to work with, the company could provide remote workers with a choice of perhaps two or three different models to choose from. Alternatively, the company may just select a model that will be provided to all remote workers.

Features to look for in a mobile phone for remote workers include:

- good battery life;
- power adapter included;
- good sound quality;
- voice messaging service;
- text messaging capability;
- synching capability.

It can be difficult to find mobile phones that don't include additional features, such as integrated cameras and MP3 players, which are not necessary for remote workers; if the selection made by the company includes those features there should be guidelines in place to cover their use.

Useful accessories

Providing a remote worker with just a laptop and sending them on their way is not going to make it easier for them to work. There are some mobile accessories that aid productivity and efficiency while working remotely.

External storage

External storage devices, whether a USB flash drive or external hard drive, are very useful for remote workers. They can be used to back up data on a regular basis to decrease the risk of data being lost or compromised.

External storage devices can also be useful for sharing data between co-workers and with customers.

Another useful feature of an external storage device is that a remote worker can store all their data on one of these and not leave it on a laptop. This way, if a laptop is lost or damaged, the data is still safe.

Optical drives

If the laptop used by remote workers does not have an integrated optical drive (CD, DVD or CD/DVD write) then providing external drives gives them another method of backing up data, creating presentations and for the installation of new applications.

An external optical drive also means that there is one less internal device that can be damaged on a laptop while travelling.

Keyboards

Your laptop keyboard may not be the most ergonomically designed device and if you work on your laptop frequently and enter a lot of information, you are very likely to experience some pain.

An external keyboard is easy to set up and use. There is a wide selection of keyboards to choose from. New laptops use USB to connect and you should be sure to plug the keyboard directly into your laptop rather than a USB hub. The keyboard you select may have specific drivers that you will be prompted for when you connect the keyboard to the laptop. It is important to note that if using an external keyboard, it is tested before working remotely with it. If the keyboard is supplied with a disk that contains special drivers it is important to install those when connecting the keyboard for the first time to ensure that the keyboard provides full functionality.

There are also wireless keyboards, which provide even more freedom to arrange your workspace.

Another advantage to using an external keyboard is that you can position the laptop at a more comfortable height and distance and place the keyboard where it is most comfortable and allows you to work safely.

Mouse

An external mouse can be a huge pain reliever as it allows more freedom of movement. While not suitable in every circumstance, most styles and connection types can be used even in tight spaces. You have a choice between a mouse that has been designed for use with a laptop or a regular mouse. A laptop mouse is smaller than a regular one but, if you find it too small and uncomfortable to use, a regular mouse will be better for your hand, wrist and shoulders.

Graphic tablets

Graphic tablets can be very useful, especially for those who need to work with graphics or want an alternative to using a mouse. Graphic tablets are also called drawing tablets or graphics pads. They provide a work surface for working with images, a stylus for making precise adjustments and some even include a mouse.

Graphic tablets are available in a variety of sizes and priced accordingly. The Tablets start at 4″ × 5″ and go as large as 9″ × 12″. Graphic tablets connect to your laptop by either USB or Bluetooth™.

If you do or plan to do a lot of work with images or drawing programs, a graphic tablet is a wise investment.

Speakers

External speakers are useful when you need to share presentations or participate in video conferencing and want better sound than headphones or the onboard speakers provide.

You have a choice between speakers designed specifically for laptops or you can use standard desktop computer speakers. If you are responsible for presentations and ensuring that groups of people can hear what is coming from your laptop – go with high quality desktop speakers.

Headphones

Headphones are especially useful while travelling. You don't have to share what you are listening to with your neighbours and it allows for a little more privacy. There are a great many styles of headphones to choose from including earbud, over-the-head and wireless. Selecting a headphone is a personal decision as it is based on the user's comfort.

Microphones

These are quite useful when conferencing or creating audio to accompany a presentation. There are combination headphone/microphones that are very comfortable.

8. ALL THE RIGHT GEAR

Power protection

All remote workers should be provided with or have portable surge protectors and portable UPS devices. Protecting mobile equipment from power surges or fluctuations while travelling is not only a way to protect the mobile equipment itself but also provides additional protection for data. Surge protection and protection from power failures is just as important as the firewall, anti-virus and spyware protection. One surge or complete power failure can cause permanent damage to your mobile gear.

Surge protectors

It may not be possible to avoid working during inclement weather, so ensuring that remote workers use surge protectors and UPS devices can enable them to continue working without fear of loss or damage to data.

Power surges can also be caused by the electrical supply in our homes and hotel rooms, which may not always be up to date or have proper shielding from interference in place.

Surge protectors are reasonably priced, although good quality ones will not be found at discount-type stores. In any case, cost should never be a reason to not have one or more. Surge protectors should offer the following:

- insurance coverage for damage to attached equipment;
- protection from lightening strikes;
- include phone line jacks and cable connections.

Uninterruptible power supply (UPS)

This is a box-like device that you plug into a wall outlet and then plug your mobile equipment into. A UPS device will provide additional power to your equipment in the event of a power failure and allow you time to properly shut down your equipment.

Faxing

Faxing requires a remote worker to have available a data/phone modem – either integrated or external – on their laptop or desktop computer.

Faxing is a great way to share documents without having to leave a huge paper trail. Rather than printing and mailing parcels and incurring the expenses involved, it can be much easier for remote workers to fax their documentation. Faxing is also a much quicker alternative.

Portable printers, scanners and digital cameras

Mobile printers

Additional mobile peripherals that enhance remote workers' ability to work while on the road and reduce their reliance on using outside services will benefit all sides. However, it is important that companies

8. ALL THE RIGHT GEAR

avoid the temptation to purchase every device targeted to the remote work environment that comes onto the market.

There are a variety of mobile printers available, from those that can print full colour photos to those that use thermal paper. Remember the first fax machines and the slick paper that they used that came on rolls? That is thermal paper and there are portable printers that still use this type of paper. It is more expensive than regular bond paper and can be harder to locate.

As with all other mobile equipment, the job functions of the remote worker should be evaluated before investing in a mobile printer. Knowing the purpose for which the remote worker will be using the printer will help in selecting the right printer – for example, thermal printers are good for printing invoices but not photos or lengthy documents that need to be retained for longer periods of time.

Mounting a printer inside a vehicle is not cheap, nor is it practicable (the printer will require an external power source) or safe – it is not easy to keep the printer out of sight once it has been mounted.

Another factor to consider is the security and safety of printed materials. Can all remote workers guarantee that any documents they print will always be kept secure, even when out of their sight? What standards will a company adopt to ensure that printed materials are protected and how will they enforce these standards?

Above all, mobile printing is more expensive than using a standard printer and should be avoided where possible, as this is one area where companies can effectively keep printing costs down for remote workers. The initial purchase price of a quality mobile printer and the consumables can add up. It is also tempting for the remote worker to print more often when the printer is readily available. Mobile printing should be limited to documents such as forms, which require a signature or hard copies, which need to be left with clients. Alternatives to mobile printing are faxing (see above) and scanning (see below).

Portable scanners

There are a variety of portable scanners available, from those that can scan photos only, to sheet-fed scanners. There are also pen-sized scanners, which can be used to scan documents or photos.

Scanners tend to be an expensive mobile accessory and should be provided only to those remote workers who need to be able to save information that cannot be photographed or copied using any other method. However, the initial cost of this type of equipment needs to be balanced against the money it can save the company by reducing dependence on faxing. Documents can be scanned and sent by email and this reduces the amount of paper that remote workers need to carry.

Scanners also play a role in helping a remote worker to keep their documents and files organized more easily.

Digital cameras

Digital cameras can be found on mobile phones and stand-alone devices. The quality of digital cameras varies greatly from one manufacturer to another and, even for remote workers used to using traditional SLR film cameras, using a digital SLR can be a steep learning curve. Unless training is provided, a remote worker could spend more time learning by trial and error than being productive.

As technology is constantly evolving and there are new devices coming onto the market every week, what is most important is knowing the job functions of remote workers, what work results are expected of them and evaluating mobile equipment and accessories to find the best matches for each remote worker.

Software 9

Selecting the right software will enable remote workers to be more productive and prevent compatibility problems with co-workers and clients. Software programs help provide mobile connections and enable remote workers to print, fax and share files. Companies need to know why these programs should be used and in what circumstances.

Companies should note that not all programs will work the same way on all computer systems and unless they plan to purchase the latest laptops with the highest specifications, they may have to select software that will run based on the lowest system requirements. There is no sense spending a huge budget on software that only a portion of the remote workforce can use.

Other points to bear in mind when choosing software are:

- compatibility with existing programs on other computers either at home or at work;
- ease of use.

This chapter provides an overview of software programs, their features that make them smart choices for remote workers and methods to keep mobile equipment running smoothly.

Remote access software

There are a variety of software programs available for enabling remote access of computers. Programs such as these let remote workers connect to their desktop computer at home or in the office to access files, programs and even email.

Companies should review a variety of remote access programs in order to see which will offer the most features to their remote workforce. If a company elects to purchase a subscription-based service or pay-per-use service, they should make sure that there are no limits that could affect when remote workers can access their designated remote machine. Most remote access programs offer trial periods, and companies should take advantage of these trials in order to evaluate which programs have the best features to match their needs.

It should be pointed out that when remotely accessing another computer, the computer being linked to must be left on in order for the remote access to work. Some companies may have concerns about leaving unattended computers left on, especially when the office is empty.

If remote workers will need access to on-site computers while they are travelling, then before a remote worker leaves the office they should turn on the computer they will need to access and then activate password protection for the screensaver. The screensaver should be set to begin running at the shortest period (normally 1 minute). The display can also be turned off, as it is not required for remote access to work. Not only does that help it consume less power but makes it less obvious that a computer is still on.

Features to look for in remote access programs include the following.

- **Ease of use** – Remote workers don't have time to spend learning complicated programs or programs that require numerous stages to connect to the computer or network.
- **Price** – Paying the highest price for programs won't always guarantee that the program will work for remote workers. The same can be said for free programs. Strive to find a happy medium.
- **Customer support** – Companies that offer 24/7 customer service support are best suited to companies with remote workers as problems may arise outside 'traditional' business hours.
- **User opinion** – Talk with personnel from other companies to get their opinions and reviews.

Contact management software

Contact management software is usually a suite of programs that allow users to keep track of customers, schedule appointments, keep calendars, create 'to do' lists, generate reports and access their email program using the information within to create mail merges and other quickly formatted emails.

Rather than running numerous small programs or having remote workers using different programs, contact management software can be purchased for all employees and then everyone will have a common way to share information.

Many companies and remote workers don't realize the value that using a dedicated contact management software offers. These programs can normally be used with a variety of email programs and some can even work with different operating systems. There are even some contact management programs that can be synched with portable devices.

Not using contact management software means that remote workers will need to try to keep their email programs organized and then use a database or spreadsheet program to create lists and reports for their activities. This can result in each remote worker having their own method of record keeping and this can make it difficult to keep everyone on the same page when sharing information.

Free-standing contact management programs make it easy to organize customers and appointments, create reports and prepare mailings. There are often learning curves involved with these programs and if training sessions are available, it is advisable that all remote workers should attend. Training sessions will better prepare remote workers as they can learn basic troubleshooting tips and techniques to get the most from the program.

9. SOFTWARE

Synchronization software

Having the ability to keep data synchronized between devices is an important feature for remote workers. They may not use their laptop or PDA exclusively and will need a method for keeping all sources of data up to date, and reflect any changes that have been made on all sources.

Remote workers must train themselves to set a regular schedule for keeping their mobile equipment synchronized. This will help protect data and ensure that all their devices have the most up-to-date information.

Keeping two or more laptops or a combination of laptops and desktops synchronized can be done quite easily by using an external storage device and then dragging and dropping the files into the appropriate file locations on the other machine.

Companies that decide to purchase synchronization software at the corporate level should ensure that the program can be used easily, requires minimal training and the product provides a good technical support system when or if needed.

If companies decide to allow individual remote workers to purchase or obtain their own programs they should remind the remote workers to be careful about the types of programs they select and install. They should take measures not to install programs laden with spyware, malware or adware.

File sharing

There are legitimate reasons for companies to have the resources available to enable file sharing between remote workers, the corporate office and even some customers.

The simplest and most common method of file sharing is email. Remote workers can use their email to send files back and forth but this can be very cumbersome and large documents or files can easily overload a mail system.

There are companies online that offer a variety of file sharing options including the capability for remote workers to collaborate on files and documents. These types of programs provide a secure and legal way for files to be shared and worked on by any number of remote workers. They offer packages based on different requirements and types of programs, such as web conferencing, document sharing and collaboration.

Companies should investigate options that can be integrated into their corporate intranets as this helps provide a more secure work environment.

As with any other program or software that companies are looking to purchase for their remote workers, it is important to shop around and ask plenty of questions.

Questions to ask include the following.

- Are there maximum file size limits?
- What is the maximum number of participants allowed?
- Is pricing based on monthly or yearly subscription or amount of time used?
- What type of user support is available?
- What are customer support hours?
- Is customer support/user support a pay-by-use service or included in the subscription?
- How is the information protected?
- How is access verified?
- What type of protection is in place against infected documents or files?
- How quickly can access be revoked?

Companies should take advantage of any free trials that are available from different vendors. This way they can make informed decisions and find out which programs best meet their needs and the needs of their remote workforce. Remote workers can also use these trials as a method of deciding which programs are easiest to use and require the least technical support.

Office suite packages

Office suites are a collection of programs that let you create a variety of documents and allow you to use the data you created within each of the other programs in the suite. Office suites provide you with a way to be more productive and not worry about compatibility between programs.

Office suites also come with pre-loaded templates that you can use within the programs and there are always more to download from the Internet.

Buying complete office suite packages for all remote workers may not be necessary as many packages contain a variety of programs that may not be needed.

Using the information gathered when reviewing the type of work remote workers do will determine which productivity programs should be provided to remote workers. For example, not all workers will need spreadsheet or database applications (these two programs normally have the highest learning curve, which means more time and expense for training) so it would make sense to purchase stand-alone products for each user.

As a minimum, remote workers will need a word processing program, presentation program and, if they work with numbers or need to keep data organized, a spreadsheet application.

Office suite components

Word processors

Word processing programs are a staple for anyone with a computer and especially with a laptop. There isn't much you can't do with a word processor – it's a program that allows you to create all kinds of documents, as well as get creative with cards and brochures.

Programs generally include a variety of templates and additional resources such as clip-art collections and access to more resources online.

Spreadsheets

Spreadsheet programs have a bit more of a learning curve than word processing programs.

They are normally used for working with data that involves numbers and financial information. While looking at lists of numbers can be intimidating, most spreadsheet applications enable the user to create more visual presentations of the information using tables and charts. Spreadsheets are also an alternative to a full-blown database program and can be used for similar purposes.

Databases

Of all the office suite programs, database programs have the steepest learning curve – perhaps because of all the different ways that you can present information and keep track of things. Database applications can also be used to share data between other applications in order to create mail-merge lists and make mailings or sending email to a large number of people more manageable. Companies should always try to spend time on training so that employees can get the most from the application. When making the decision to choose a database program the company should keep in mind what the program will be used for and what the learning curve is. Not all workers will require full-blown database applications and there are free alternatives that enable them to work with databases created in other applications. In order to learn how to use any database application and learn the versatility they offer, users should be encouraged to create dummy databases that do contain vital information but will allow them to explore the options available.

Presentation software

Presentation software enables the creator to use a more graphic application to present information. This software is also one of the easier applications to learn and use. Presentation software is an ideal application for remote workers to use to share information with others. Presentations can be posted online, sent by email, and can also be copied to CD/DVDs and will run automatically when opened. In this way the information can be shared effortlessly and this is more economical than setting up large conferences. Imagery used in presentation software can be tailored to specific audiences and provide an easier to digest view of complex data.

Free or fee?

Do you really need to pay for an office suite? There are free alternatives and it seems that more are becoming available. Free programs work well for those who don't need all the features that the paid versions offer.

Online options

There are now a variety of online alternatives to traditional office suites and this could be a very useful solution for remote workers. Online applications can be very handy for laptop users as they reduce the number of programs to install and the information created in these applications can be accessed from anywhere, which means less data to keep on your laptop.

Scanning

In addition to the scanning equipment described in the previous chapter, there is also software for scanning and there are programs that can be purchased for specific functions, such as scanning and keeping business cards organized.

Graphics

Digital photos, whether taken by a dedicated digital camera or mobile phone with integrated camera, are being used much more frequently and in a wider variety of jobs.

If high-end photo manipulation is not required, there are plenty of free or low-cost graphics applications that can be used by remote workers. In many cases, these free or low-cost programs are also much easier to use and require less hard drive space than other, more expensive alternatives.

Software updates

Updates are an important part of keeping your mobile equipment running properly. There are updates for operating systems, additional software programs you run and for hardware. You do have a choice as to how updates are handled – manual or automatic.

Automatic updates allow you to download and install new updates as they become available. You may not always know which updates are being downloaded and installed so troubleshooting a problem can be more difficult. When a new laptop is set up for the first time, you will be prompted to select automatic updates. If you are comfortable with that choice, click yes and you don't have to think about it again unless a problem occurs at some point.

Manual updates mean that you must check for updates on a regular basis and decide which ones you wish to download and install. Manual updates are better if you prefer to know what you are going to be installing. Manual updates also allow you to download and install one update at a time, restart your laptop and make sure everything still works properly. If a problem does occur, then you will know that perhaps the cause may be the update, which has caused a conflict or created a problem with another program. It is easier to track the changes and find solutions to any problems that may arise by doing updates one at a time.

A good schedule for checking updates for firewall, anti-virus and spyware is once a week. Operating system and hardware updates can be checked on a monthly basis. Keeping an eye out for news or announcements of updates is also wise. Many programs now allow you to subscribe to an update notification system.

Keeping your laptop running smoothly

Not only is it important to keep protective software up to date and used properly, but you should also make a habit of cleaning up your hard drive. This may seem time-consuming but will help keep your laptop running smoothly and put less wear and tear on the hard drive.

If you want your laptop to work properly, last for a while and not give you any problems, take the time to protect it from the start, rather than after a problem has occurred.

Scanning hard drives

Over time and after installing new programs, you may find your that your laptop has begun to slow down and programs are not running as fast as they originally did. In order to get programs running properly and regain lost hard drive space, you should scan the hard drive and defragment it so that it can reorganize itself.

Depending how large your hard drive is and how many programs you have installed, defragmentation can take anything from a few minutes to hours. Some operating systems will allow you to set a schedule for when you want your hard drive defragmented. If you set a time for this to occur then you will have to remember to leave your laptop turned on so that the program can work.

Other operating systems will allow you to correct small errors in the disk directory structure and repair file permissions for the system.

You could also go through and remove any programs or drivers for accessories that you are not using on a regular basis or were trials of programs that you forgot you had. This will help reclaim some hard drive space.

More hard drive space can be found by emptying the cache files and temporary Internet files, as well as deleting accumulated music, videos and pictures. You can also delete back-up or temporary files that have been automatically created by the system when working on documents or installing programs. You may want to back up the original file first to make sure you always have a copy available.

Successful remote working – a conclusion

10

Companies will benefit from remote working as it increases the levels of customer service that they can offer, it will allow them to reach more clients and potentially increase their customer base.

Many remote workers will have travel involved in their remote work arrangement but their travel plans can be arranged on more flexible schedules and, in some cases, with the use of the right technology, some travel can be eliminated. The Internet has opened new opportunities and methods of working remotely. A person isn't tied to a landline phone system nor must they have to sit at a desk all day from 9–5.

While there are sectors of the employed who don't understand how remote work can enhance and improve work/life balance there are others who insist on some form of remote work options.

Allowing workers to have more time to meet familial commitments results in workers that stay motivated, maintain if not improve productivity and are less likely to burn out.

The demands put upon workers by their employers and families often result in increased health concerns and problems. Relieving or lessening stress levels by changing how and where an employee works benefits everyone.

Not all companies are ready to take the plunge into remote work but when they do they must be prepared to take steps to train their employees, create usable guidelines and policies and be prepared to enforce the consequences of failing to abide by them.

In order for remote work programmes to succeed, companies must take the right steps and remember that selecting the right people – remote workers and their respective management team – and positions for remote work will lead to greater success and overall satisfaction with work and life.

Most of all, companies should take seriously the security risks that may be involved or that remote workers expose themselves to when they start out.

Work wisely, safely and enjoy your new path to success.